We All Share

PLAY
AROUND THE WORLD

BY
PATRICIA LAKIN

A BLACKBIRCH PRESS BOOK

WOODBRIDGE, CONNECTICUT

CONTENTS

Published by Blackbirch Press, Inc.
One Bradley Road
Woodbridge, CT 06525

©1995 Blackbirch Press, Inc.
First Edition

10 9 8 7 6 5 4 3 2 1

Photo Credits
Cover: ©Martin Rogers/Tony Stone Images, Inc.; Series Logo: ©Tanya Stone; p. 3: ©Bob Krist/Tony Stone Worldwide; p. 5: ©Nair Benedicto/f4/DDB Stock Photo; p. 7: ©Brian Milne/Earth Scenes; p. 8: ©Dale Boyer/Tony Stone Images; p. 9: ©Audrey Topping/Photo Researchers, Inc.; p. 11: ©Jeff Greenberg/Peter Arnold, Inc.; p. 13: ©Jeff Greenberg/Photo Researchers, Inc.; p. 15: ©Bruce Davidson/Earth Scenes; p. 17: ©Renato Rotolo/Gamma-Liaison; p. 19: ©Martha Cooper/Peter Arnold, Inc.; pp. 21, 25: ©Steve Vidler/Leo de Wys, Inc.; p. 23: ©Robert Harding/Peter Arnold, Inc.; p. 27: ©Bill Truslow/Tony Stone Worldwide; p. 29: Chad Coppess/South Dakota Tourism; p. 31: ©Dan Smith/Tony Stone Worldwide.

Library of Congress Cataloging–in–Publication Data
Lakin, Pat.
    Play / by Patricia Lakin.   —1st ed.
      p. cm.—(We all share)
    Includes bibliographical references and index.
      ISBN 1-56711-141-6
        1.Games—Cross-cultural studies—
            Juvenile literature. I. Title.
    II. Series.
    GV1203.L35 1995
    796--dc20   94-38497
                                            CIP
                                            AC

INTRODUCTION

Children around the world like to take time from their chores or from their schoolwork to do the one thing all children love: play. It can mean playing with a ball, a stick or a bat, cards, marbles, dice, an electronic game, or a pencil and paper. Sometimes kids play alone, other times they play with lots of friends. Playing pieces can come from almost anywhere; they can be bought from a store, handed down from one generation to the next, or even found around the house. The playing area can be a wide open field, a small backyard, or a city playground tucked between tall buildings.

In the following pages, you will see children and adults from many different countries at play. No matter what they are doing, or where they are doing it, it will be obvious that play is something everyone everywhere loves to do.

Play is something everyone likes to do.

BRAZIL

Brazil is the largest country in South America. Among its many important industries are leather, coffee, and beef.

Brazilian kids like to play lots of games. Kids in Brazil's big cities often play games in public playgrounds. Kids in the countryside play lots of games in wide open fields and pastures.

One of the most popular games for children in Brazil is a simple game called Peteca. The Peteca pouch is made from leather. It is stuffed with sawdust or sand to give it weight. Feathers are sewn at the top of the pouch to give it balance.

Peteca is played much the way children in other countries play with bean bags. It is like the popular bean bag game called hackeysack in North America. The object of Peteca is to hit the bag in the air as it is passed around and not let it fall to the ground.

These kids enjoy playing in a playground in Sao Paulo, one of Brazil's largest cities.

CANADA

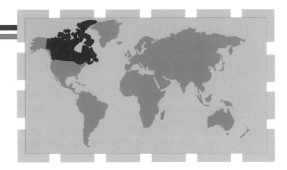

Canada is the second-largest country in the world. It is also the northernmost country in North America. In most parts of Canada, the winters are long and cold.

Whether a Canadian child lives near the Atlantic Coast, the Pacific Coast, or somewhere in between, in winter, they are not far from frozen rivers, ponds, lakes, or skating rinks. That is one of the reasons why two games played on the ice are so popular in Canada: ice hockey and curling. Curling was brought to Canada from Scotland. This game uses a 42-pound stone that has a handle on the top. The object of the game is to swing the stone down a long, rectangular ice court and get it as close to a target as possible. Curling teams are called risks. When one risk member swings the stone, another risk member is allowed to sweep a broom in front of the stone. With a swept path, the stone may get closer to the target.

A group of boys in Jasper plays hockey on one of the region's many frozen lakes.

Ice hockey was created in Canada in 1855. At a very young age, Canadian children put on their skates and go out on the ice. There, they will start hitting the hockey puck across the frozen surface.

CHINA

Located in East Asia, China is the third-largest country in the world. With its population of more than 1 billion, China contains one fourth of the world's people.

The Chinese have traditionally liked to play card or board games. One game is a Chinese version of chess. Another is a "strategy" board game that has been around for thousands of years. It is called "Go," or Wequi. Wequi was created over 2,000 years ago, but is still a very popular game today. It is played with black and white pieces. The board is divided into 19 horizontal and 19 vertical lines. The object is for one player to capture the other player's squares or territories.

Round pieces are arranged on a large board in the Chinese version of chess.

Mah-Jongg is another game that was created in
China. It is played with beautifully engraved white
tiles. The tiles are the same shape as the tiles in
dominoes. Mah-Jongg, however, is really more closely
related to the popular American card game, Rummy.

RUSSIA

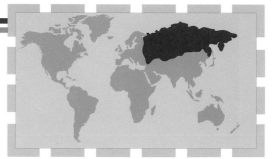

Russia, in Asia, is the largest country in the world. Its boundaries cover more than 6.5 million square miles.

Children in many countries around the world like to play chess. But in Russia, the majority of children learn to play this complicated, two-person board game at a very early age.

A chess board has alternating squares in two different colors. There are also chess pieces of each color, with six different kinds of figures for each player to move, including a king. Each figure can only move a certain way and a certain number of squares. The object of the game is to capture, or trap, the opponent's king.

Along with a chess set, a Russian child's room most probably also contains a Matreshka doll. This small doll is pear-shaped and is made out of hollowed-out wood. The outside is brightly colored and is usually painted to look like a Russian peasant. What is so special about this doll is that there are more dolls inside. When someone twists a Matreshka near its waist, the doll comes apart. Inside is an identically painted, but slightly smaller, doll! In an instant, a Russian boy or girl can have a whole family of dolls! There can be as many as 11 dolls hiding inside one Matreshka.

Boys in downtown Moscow play a game of cards together.

MEXICO

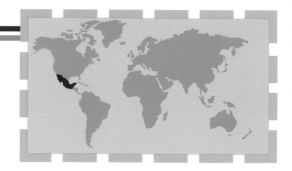

Mexico is a Spanish-speaking country that borders the southern United States. Because Mexico is close to the equator, this country has many months of warm, sunny days.

Outdoor games can be played by Mexican children all year long. One of the most popular, especially for Mexican children who do not live in a city, is Canicas. It is a glass marble game played on the ground.

In Canicas, children divide into two teams. If possible, each team has its own color of marble. The players prepare the ground by digging a small hole. The object of the game is very much like golf—each

Mexican kids show some American visitors how to play Canicas.

player must roll the marble into the hole in as few tries as possible. The team with more of their marbles in the hole at the end of the game is the winner!

KENYA

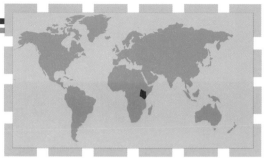

Kenya is located on the eastern coast of Africa. It borders Somalia. The equator— an imaginary line that divides the globe into north and south—runs through the middle of the country.

In many African countries, children enjoy playing a mathematical game called Mancala. In Kenya, the game is called Wari.

The two-player game of Wari is very easy to learn, but takes some time and thought to become a skilled player. Wari is played with beans or seeds and a wooden board with four or five carved-out pits on each side. At either end of the board is a "home" pit for each player. Each player takes turns scooping out the seeds or beans from one pit on their side of the board. Without skipping a pit, they must go counter-clockwise and drop one seed or bean into each of the following pits until the seeds or beans in the player's hand are gone. The object of the game is to get the most seeds or beans into the player's "home" pit.

A young boy in Kenya plays a fence-post game similar to the American game of tag.

ITALY

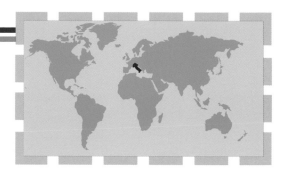

Italy is a long, skinny peninsula of rugged beauty. A peninsula is a land mass that is surrounded by water on all sides but one. Italy has France, Austria, and Switzerland on its northern borders.

Like people in many other European countries, Italians love to play soccer. (In Europe, soccer is actually called football.) As the most popular sport in the world, soccer has attracted well over a billion fans around the globe.

Soccer is a fast-paced game of running and nonstop action. The rules of the game are fairly simple, and very little equipment is needed. Soccer is played with a leather or rubber ball that is a little smaller than a basketball. A soccer field is usually about the size of an American football field. The object of the game is to move the ball to the opposing team's goal and to get the ball past the goalie that guards the area. The ball can be moved by kicking, headbutting, or hitting with any part of the body other than the hands.

Soccer requires a great deal of running and stop-and-start movement. Because of this, good soccer players must be in top physical condition. The best thing about soccer, however, is that almost anyone can play—whatever their skill level may be.

Two young girls from Apulia take a break from playing on the cobblestone streets of their town.

ISRAEL

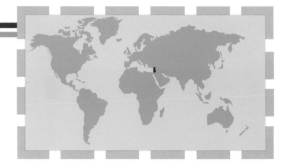

Israel is a tiny country in the Middle East. Much of Israel is desert. But with irrigation systems bringing in water, this country has become one of the largest producers of peaches, citrus, and other fruits.

Before electronic games took up Israeli children's playtime, they used peach pits to make a toy and create a game.

The toy is a self-made whistle. Each end of the peach pit is dipped in water and then rubbed along a rough surface until a little hole is made at either end of the pit. When air is blown into one end, it makes the inner peach pit vibrate. This vibration creates a whistling noise.

The word *gogoem* actually means "peach pits." Gogoem is played by any number of children. To play the game, children stand in front of a wall and draw boundary areas close to the wall. Each player uses a stick to hit peach pits against the wall. The object of the game is to hit the pits hard enough so that they hit the wall and fall to the ground, close to the wall, and inside the boundary. The winner is the player with the most peach pits inside his or her boundary.

Two boys in Jerusalem use a homemade cart to play on the city's sidewalk.

EGYPT

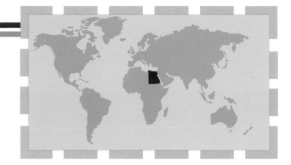

Egypt is a large country on the northern coast of the African continent. Much of Egypt is desert, but there are many large cities, too.

Egyptian children—like many children around the world—love marble games! A favorite game of Egyptian children, especially those who live in rural areas, is called Bely. It is played on the ground. Two or more players aim and roll their marbles and try to hit a target marble.

Unlike the Mexican marble game of Canicas, Bely is played more like a bowling game. Marble games and the game of bowling were believed to have started in Egypt thousands of years ago!

Right: A group of Egyptian boys plays soccer in front of one of the country's many giant pyramids.

PAKISTAN

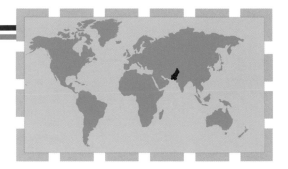

Pakistan is a small country in Asia that is bordered by India on the east. Up until 1947, Pakistan was part of India. Now, they are two separate countries.

Two popular Pakistani games are played by children around the world. The first, called Guli Danda, is a simple game, but it takes a great deal of practice and hand-eye coordination to master. It consists of two sticks. One stick is thin and long and is used like a bat. The second stick is much shorter, has a whittled-down point, and is used like a ball. Children in Pakistan take the short stick and place it on the edge of a table or on a rock. With the longer stick, they quickly whack the shorter stick and send it flying up into the air. In a flash, they use that same long stick to try to bat at the airborne stick.

In America, the game is called Peggy and is played with a stick and a whittled-down wooden clothes pin.

The second game popular with Pakistani children is a board game called Ludo. This game is also known as Pahcheesi and was created in India. Ludo is a strategic board game for two, three, or four players. Each player must move all of his or her four wooden discs, or men, around the game board and try not to get captured. The first player to get all four of his or her men "home" is the winner.

Schoolkids in Islamabad play together on their playground jungle gym.

GREECE

Greece is a rugged and dramatic country on the Mediterranean Ocean. In between what is formally considered Europe and the Middle East, Greece's culture blends influences from both.

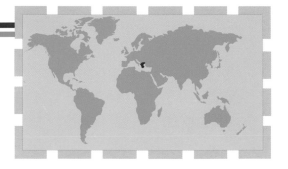

In Ancient Greece, children played a game called Tsiliki, or jacks. They used small animal bones as the playing pieces. Today in Greece, and around the world, the game is played with metal jacks and a ball. The rules, however, are the same everywhere. The jacks are thrown onto a smooth surface like a table top or a floor. A player then tosses a small ball into the air. Before the ball is caught by the player, he or she must pick up a certain number of jacks without touching or moving the other jacks in the pile. If the jacks in the pile are moved or the ball is not caught, the player's turn ends and another player gets a turn. The winner is the first player who successfully goes through all the steps of the game.

A girl in traditional costume takes part in a celebration of Greek culture.

UNITED STATES

The United States is the fourth-largest country in the world. Together with Canada, it makes up most of North America.

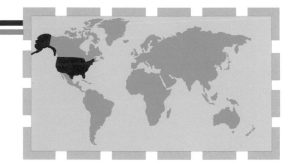

The game of baseball is known in America as the "national pastime." That is because many young Americans will play the game at one time or another as they grow up.

To play baseball, two teams of nine players each face off on a diamond-shaped field. One team takes the field while the other team sends its players up to bat one at a time. The players, batting at home plate, try to hit the ball hard enough or far enough so they can run around the three bases and wind up back at home plate. Each time a player returns to home plate, a run is scored. The team with the most runs at the end of the game is the winner.

The game of baseball actually grew out of the popular British games of cricket and rounders. These games are also played with a bat and a ball. Baseball has played a major part in the creation of American culture. The game has provided the country with many great heroes and role models.

Baseball has also been the subject of countless popular movies, books, and songs.

Baseball is known as the "American national pastime."

NATIVE AMERICAN

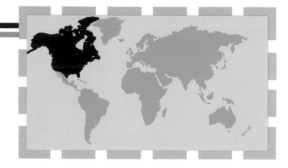

Many different Native American tribes have inhabited what is now North America for thousands of years.

Far before any Europeans landed on North American soil, the various native peoples who lived on the North American continent created and played an outdoor game that is still played today. It is now known as lacrosse. This game is popular with many children, especially in Canada and along the East Coast of the United States.

The game is played much like it was hundreds of years ago. There is a goal on either end of a large playing field. Each player has a long stick, or crosse. There is a small net, or face, at the end of each crosse. A hard, rubber ball, slightly smaller than a baseball, is scooped or caught into the net and thrown from it. Players run up and down the field tossing the ball back and forth from their nets. The object of the game is to get the ball into the opponent's goal.

Young Native Americans from South Dakota rest in the shade after playing a game of basketball.

UNITED KINGDOM

The United Kingdom (UK)—which includes England, Scotland, Wales, and Northern Ireland—is a group of islands in Northern Europe. Off the northwestern coast of mainland Europe, the UK shares a great deal with its neighbors across the English Channel.

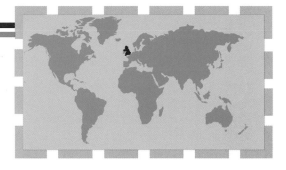

Rugby is one of the most popular games in the UK. It is also the direct ancestor of American football. Like American football, rugby is a kicking, passing, and tackling game that is played on a grass field. Even the ball that is used looks almost exactly like an American football. Unlike the American game, however, no heavy padding or helmets are worn in rugby.

Rugby can be said to be the British "national pastime" in the same way that baseball is the American pastime. Most young boys in the United Kingdom will play rugby at one time or another as they grow up.

A mud-soaked boy carries the rugby ball as he runs down the field.

GLOSSARY

crosse The stick used in the game of lacrosse.

equator An imaginary line around the earth that divides the globe into north and south.

irrigation A system that brings water through land to feed plants and crops.

pastime Recreation.

peninsula A land form surrounded by water on three sides.

risk Curling team.

INDEX